"This has rapidly become one of the most beloved books in our home. My kids loved it and asked me to read it over and over again!"

LAURA WIFLER, Founder and Executive Director, Risen Motherhood

"Superb storytelling, fantastic illustrations, and a message every parent will want their kids to hear. I'm not sure who will love it more—your kids hearing it, or you reading it to them!"

J.D. GREEAR, Pastor, The Summit Church, Durham, North Carolina

"Good children's books are easy for everyone to understand. The best children's books leave everyone (the reader and the one being read to) in awe. That's what *The God Contest* does. It's not just the truth that shines through; it's the beauty. This is how we cultivate the seeds of faith in the soil of our children's hearts."

JOHN ONWUCHEKWA, Lead Pastor, Cornerstone Church Atlanta; Author, *Prayer*

"A child's experience in seasons of uncertainty may differ than that of an adult, though we all need to rest in the same assurance: Christ is victorious. *The God Contest* serves all of us in these beautifully illustrated and faithfully retold accounts of how God demonstrates his mighty power for his glory and our eternal good."

GLORIA FURMAN, Author, *Missional Motherhood* and *Labor With Hope*

"A bright and lively version of one of the most dramatic stories in the Bible, with super illustrations and a great punchline. What's not to like?!"

ANDREW AND RACHEL WILSON, Authors, *The Life We Never Expected*

"When it comes to telling kids how wonderful, powerful and real God is, my friend Carl takes the prize—and he does it with words that sing and shine the truth. Even the whimsical illustrations grip the imagination! *The God Contest* will indelibly impress the timeless story of Elijah on Mt. Carmel upon the heart of every young reader. I love this book, and I give it a double thumbs-up!"

JONI EARECKSON TADA, Joni and Friends Disability Center

thegoodbook
for children

The God Contest
© The Good Book Company / Catalina Echeverri 2021. Reprinted 2021 (three times), 2022 (twice).

Illustrated by Catalina Echeverri | Design & Art Direction by André Parker

"The Good Book For Children" is an imprint of The Good Book Company Ltd
North America: thegoodbook.com UK: thegoodbook.co.uk Australia: thegoodbook.com.au
New Zealand: thegoodbook.co.nz India: thegoodbook.co.in

ISBN: 9781784984786 | Printed in India

THE GOD CONTEST

CARL LAFERTON

CATALINA ECHEVERRI

THE TRUE STORY OF
ELIJAH, JESUS, AND THE
GREATEST VICTORY

There are all sorts of contests.

Spelling contests.

Singing contests.

Sewing contests.

Sporting contests.

But this book isn't about any of those contests...

It's about the God contest—a challenge to find out who the real God was.

Ahab and Jezebel were King and Queen of Israel.

They thought Baal was the real God.

They said Baal made food grow.

They said Baal made babies grow.

They said Baal was super-powerful.

Loads of people joined Team Baal.

Elijah was just an ordinary guy. He told the people of Israel that Yahweh* was the real God, and that he was one of Yahweh's messengers.

Elijah said Yahweh had made everything and ruled everywhere and loved everyone. He said Yahweh had rescued their great-great-great-great-great-great-grandparents from Egypt. He said Yahweh had given them their land and their laws.

But not many people joined Team Yahweh.

*In the Old Testament of most English Bibles, it says "LORD" wherever the first Old Testaments, written thousands of years ago, said "Yahweh."

Most people didn't know *which* God
to believe in.

Maybe Baal was the real God.
Maybe Yahweh was.
Maybe both of them were.
Maybe neither of them were...

How could they decide?

Elijah had a good idea. It was time for a contest. A God contest, on a mountain called Mount Carmel...

All the people came to watch the God contest.
Elijah said to them,

"How long are you going to take to make up
your mind? If Yahweh is God, then follow
him. But if Baal is God, then follow him.
It's time to decide."

Elijah explained the rules:

"I'll chop up some wood, and some people from Team Baal can chop up some wood. We'll each put a dead bull on our wood. Then they can ask Baal to prove himself, and I'll ask Yahweh to prove himself.

"The God who can set the bull on fire—he's the real God. He'll be the winner of the God contest."

Team Baal went first. 450 of them shouted to Baal.
They kept shouting to Baal. They shouted to Baal for hours.

Nothing happened.

They danced around their wood. They kept dancing around
their wood. They danced around their wood for hours.

Nothing happened.

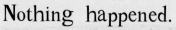

Elijah teased them:

"Maybe you need to shout louder. Maybe Baal is busy thinking. Maybe he's on the toilet. Maybe he's away from home. Maybe he's asleep."

Team Baal shouted louder and louder and louder.
From lunchtime till nighttime, they shouted.
No answer. No fire. Nothing happened at all.

Then it was Elijah's turn.
He was the only one on Team Yahweh.

He dug a trench
around his wood.

He poured water
all over everything
until the trench
was full and
everything was
completely wet.

There was no way it
could be set on fire.

Then Elijah spoke
to Yahweh...

"Yahweh, please make it clear today that you are God.
Please answer me, Yahweh, so that all these people
will know that you are the only real God, and that
you want them to follow you and love you."

And...

The fire burned the bull.
The fire burned the wood.
The fire burned the water.

The people knew who had
won the God contest.

But...

King Ahab and Queen Jezebel didn't like the result. So they decided to carry on following the made-up god, Baal.

And the people soon forgot the result too. They didn't remember that Yahweh is the real God, the only God, the God who made everything and rules everywhere and loves everyone, the God who sent the fire on the mountain. For hundreds of years, not many people joined Team Yahweh.

It was time for another God contest.

This time, Yahweh did something even more amazing.

He didn't send fire.
He came as a human...

JESUS.

Jesus said he was Yahweh.

Jesus showed he was Yahweh.

But people weren't sure.

Maybe Jesus was the real God.
But maybe he wasn't.
Maybe there were lots of gods.
Or maybe there was no God at all.

How could they decide?

It was time for a final God contest, on another mountain, called Mount Zion.

Jesus explained the rules:

"I will come back to life after I have died.
Then you'll Know I'm Yahweh. And then I'll
give life forever to everyone who is on my team."

So Jesus let people kill him, on a cross.

Jesus was placed in a tomb on the side of the mountain.

He was completely dead. There was no way he could ever be alive again.

And for three days, nothing happened.

It looked like Jesus had lost the God contest.

And then...

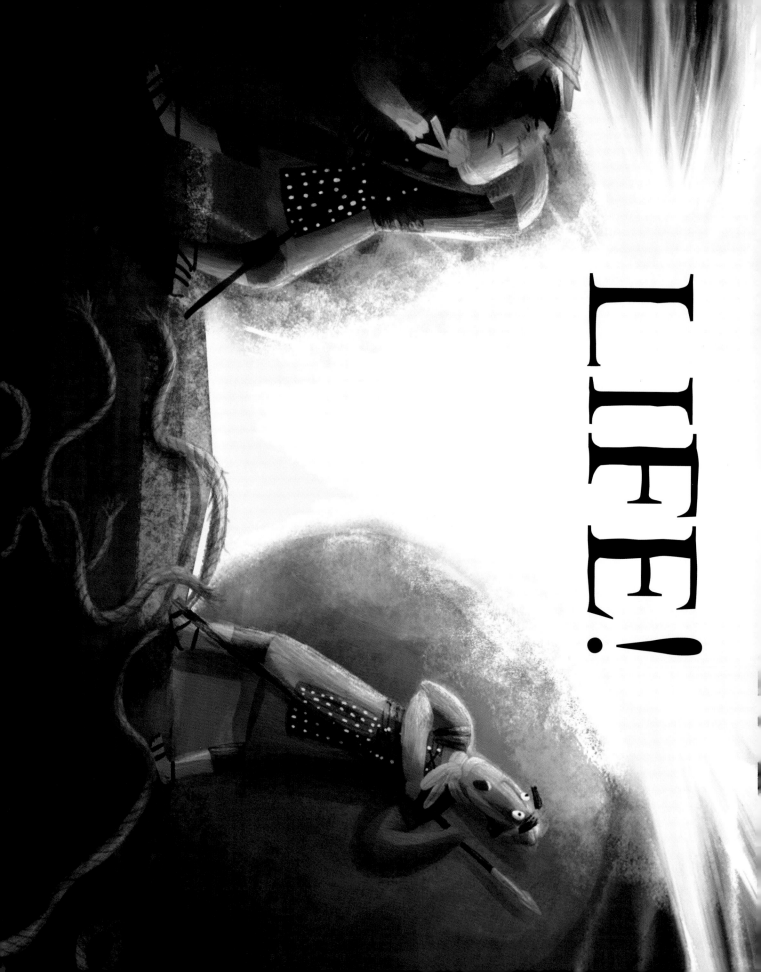

Jesus rose back to life.
Jesus had a body that worked.
Jesus could live forever.
 The God contest was over.

JESUS is YAHw

PHOEBE   THOMAS   PERPETUA   ATHANASIUS   AUGUSTINE of HIPPO   CLOTILDE of BURGUNDY   ANSELM of CANTERBURY   MARTIN LUTHER and KATHARINA VON BORA   ANNE ASKEW   GEORGE WHITEFIELD

Now lots of people knew that Jesus was the real God, the only God, the God who made everything and rules everywhere and loves everyone and could give them life forever.

Now lots of people said...

EH, JESUS is GOD!

Now lots of people joined Team Jesus.

MUEL HAYNES   HUDSON TAYLOR   BETSEY STOCKTON   AMY CARMICHAEL   BETTY STAM   BROTHER YUN   ELISABETH ELLIOT   MAHALIA JACKSON   FRANCIS SCHAEFFER

But not everyone did.

    Some people didn't like the result.
                Some people still don't.

    Some people didn't remember the result.
                Some people still don't.

But Jesus did win
the God contest.

Jesus did rise back to
life from the dead.

Jesus did prove that he's the real God, the only God, who
wants everyone to follow him as their ruler and love
him as their rescuer and enjoy life forever with him.

So everybody has to make their minds up.
Will they join Team Jesus?

What will you decide?

HOW DO WE KNOW ABOUT
THE GOD CONTEST?

Elijah lived during a time of crisis for the people of God. Centuries before, they had been rescued from Egypt by God, who had introduced himself by his personal name: Yahweh or "I AM WHO I AM" (see Exodus 3 v 1-15—English Bibles tend to translate Yahweh as "LORD"). Yahweh had given them a land to live in and godly kings to rule them. But by Elijah's time the rulers and people had begun to worship and serve the made-up gods of the surrounding nations, such as the Canaanite god Baal. As Yahweh's prophet, Elijah was sent to call the people back to worshipping Yahweh.

The "God contest" on Mount Carmel is recorded in 1 Kings 18 v 16-40. Afterwards, Queen Jezebel tried to kill Elijah, and most of the people forgot what they had seen (19 v 1-2, 9b-10). After Elijah went to heaven, centuries passed before Yahweh came himself as a man called Jesus, who died on a cross and then rose from a tomb on Mount Zion (Luke 24 v 1-8)—the greatest proof of all that Yahweh is truly God, and that Jesus is Yahweh. Amazingly though, Elijah and Jesus did actually meet in this world, on top of another mountain—which you can read about in Luke 9 v 28-36.